PENNSYLVANIA'S LANDMARKS

TABLE OF CONTENTS

French Azilum
A pastoral refuge fit for the Queen of France — 27

Anthracite Museum Complex
Four sites that tell the story of days when coal was king — 28

Two Museums of Industry
Museums that tell of two historically important industries — 29

Cornwall Iron Furnace
Site of cannon production for the Revolution — 30

Hopewell Village National Historic Site
A complete ironmaking community — 32

Drake Well Museum
The site of the world's first oil well — 33

State Museum of Pennsylvania
Industry, transport, arts, natural history, and culture on exhibit — 34

Union Canal Tunnel
A link in the connection of the Schuylkill to the Susquehanna — 36

Allegheny Portage Railroad
Pennsylvania Canal link that carried freight over the mountain — 37

Gettysburg National Military Park
The battle that turned the tide in America's Civil War — 38

Flagship Niagara
A reconstructed War of 1812 brig on Lake Erie — 40

Pottsgrove Manor
Ironmaster's home and its 18th-century furnishings — 41

Historic Lancaster
The Fulton Opera House and President Buchanan's Wheatland — 42

East Broad Top Railroad
Narrow-gauge coal-hauling railroad, now an excursion road — 43

Historic Bethlehem
The Christmas City, where Moravian culture prospered — 44

Pennsylvania Military Museum
Where the tradition of Pennsylvania's men-at-arms is kept alive — 46

Bushy Run Battlefield
Commemorating a decisive action in the Indian wars — 47

Map of Pennsylvania's Historic Sites — 48

LOCATION: Bucks County, near U.S. 1 and 13, south of Morrisville
PENNSBURY MANOR

Pennsbury Manor

The home of William Penn, beautifully re-created, a monument to the founder of Pennsylvania

The reconstruction of William Penn's glorious country home is a fitting memorial to a giant among the founders of the English colonies in America. Paradoxically, Penn lived in the house for less than two years, but his devotion to it is evidenced by the instructions concerning its design and construction which he wrote from England during his residence there between 1684 and 1699.

Dissenter in Religion

Penn's first acquaintance with dissenting doctrines in religion was at Oxford. An early sympathy for the Society of Friends was later confirmed in his encounters in Ireland with the Quaker preacher Thomas Loe. William's Quaker beliefs conflicted with the Church of England to the distress of the lad's father, Sir William, whose naval career and friendship with the king thrust him into the alliance of religion and class—of churchman and aristocrat, puritan and merchant, and dissenter and commoner—that had vexed and divided the English.

On the one hand king and bishops upheld tradition, while on the other their opponents—Quakers among them—were drawn to the vision of a new order grounded on the Biblical promise of "new heavens and a new earth." Consequently, nonconformists suffered restrictions placed upon accepted liberties, and while many were enduring a life of hardship, young Penn was sent to France for a taste of the world, and to Ireland to renegotiate rental agreements for the family estate. Inspired there by his newfound faith, Penn preached, wrote and defended the Society of Friends despite arrest and trial.

Reformer in Government

Although he believed that nations and governments would eventually be similarly inspired, it seemed more promising to incorporate his vision of liberty into the embryonic society of the New World than to persist in an attempt to reform the rigid order of the old.

Penn's plan was accepted by his father's friend, King Charles II, who saw the intended change of residence of the brilliant young Quaker as a solution to the problem of conflict that could arise between the authorities and those for whom England had become a troubled place of residence. He, therefore, chartered the admiral's son as Proprietor of a substantial but unoccupied tract of land to which the Crown lay claim, named it Pennsylvania, and thus dealt with two thorny problems in one brilliant stroke of the royal pen. The year was 1681.

Invitation to Citizenship

Penn expected—rather hoped, it is assumed—to have a Quaker majority in his new domain. But true to his religious principles, he was glad to accept anyone who believed in God. All were to have the liberties of Englishmen plus citizenship in a land where "laws rule and the people are a party to them." But all who were tempted to accept this offer were also warned that there was to be "no pretence of conscience to be drunk, to whore, to be voluptuous, to game, to swear, curse, blaspheme, and profane." The punishment of crime was to be milder than that provided by the harsh penal code of England, and on two key points of Quaker belief, neither swearing of oaths nor bearing of arms was to be required of citizens.

Settlers—for the most part shopkeepers, artisans, manual workers and their families—began to arrive at Chester in 1681. Penn himself reached the New World in October, 1682, aboard the ship *Welcome*. A third of the passengers had died of smallpox during the voyage.

Triumph and Defeat

After only two years William Penn was forced to return to England and the royal court to protect his interests and to settle a boundary dispute with Maryland. Despite his intention to return soon to America with his wife and children, he was delayed for 15 years. Gulielma eventually died in 1699 and Penn remarried. His new wife, Hannah Callowhill, eventually the mother of seven, returned with him in 1699.

By this time his house was completed, gardens were installed, and a staff of servants and African slaves was assembled to care for the home and surrounding fields. During the two summers he spent in the house, Penn was beset with the problems of taxation and the enforcement of trade and navigation laws. It is certain that Penn was a deeply troubled man, struggling against great odds to build a just and harmonious society in his Commonwealth, one that anticipated and influenced the fundamental features of American life—religious freedom, popular government and a sense of world mission.

Decline and Rebirth

Clear title to Pennsbury Manor was in doubt after the American Revolution and, without occupants, the house eventually sank into ruins, with only the foundations and part of an outbuilding surviving into the 1830's.

Reconstruction, begun by the Commonwealth in the late 1930's, was made difficult by the total absence of original architectural drawings, and was surrounded by controversy since so little could be proved of the actual design of the original structure. Archeological work, plus gleanings from Penn's correspondence, gave architect R. Brognard Okie a basis for his work. Beyond that slim basis the creation has been both criticized as a dream and praised as a fitting memorial, whatever its underlying authenticity.

Pennsbury Manor kitchen

LOCATION: One mile north of U. S. 422 at Baumstown, Berks County

DANIEL BOONE HOMESTEAD

A mid-18th-century stone farmhouse, built on the site of the log cabin that was Daniel Boone's Birthplace

Daniel Boone was born in 1734 in Berks County, Pennsylvania, the sixth of 11 children of weaver and blacksmith Squire Boone and his wife, Sarah Morgan. Boone's Quaker parents had traveled from Devonshire, England, to Pennsylvania and purchased 250 acres in Montgomery County, where they built a log house on a stone foundation at the edge of the wilderness. It was here that young Daniel is said to have first learned marksmanship, probably with an English fowling piece, later to be perfected in his use of a long Pennsylvania rifle.

The Boones Move On

In 1750, possibly as a result of a controversy with the elders of their Quaker meeting, the Boones began a trek that took them to Maryland, Virginia, and their final place of settlement, North Carolina.

Six years later, at the age of 21, Daniel married 16-year-old Rebecca Bryan. Their union brought ten children, despite many periods of lonely separation as Daniel's restless spirit took him farther and farther to the west. Each time, Daniel returned to move his family to the new lands he had explored.

Daniel Boone in Kentucky

It was the Bluegrass region of Kentucky that ultimately captured Daniel's restless spirit, plunging him into further explorations, war with the Indians, and additional incredible adventures. Daniel's attempts at business were less successful than the more physical undertakings of his youth, and in 1799, at the age of 65, having given up all of his holdings to satisfy a mountain of debt, Daniel moved his family to Missouri at the invitation of the Spanish governor. He died at the age of 85 in 1820.

The Homestead

The original Boone log house, located east of Reading in Berks County, was replaced in the 18th century by a stone structure, although the original cellar and spring make up part of the present house. The site is arranged to interpret the Boone family and two later families by telling the story of early settlement and the diversity of this Pennsylvania region. A smokehouse, blacksmith shop, barn, and Bertolet log house and sawmill are open to the public.

The stone farmhouse, one of several buildings open to the public at the Daniel Boone Homestead east of Reading

LOCATION: Near the Delaware, a few blocks from the junction of PA 291 and PA 420.

MORTON HOMESTEAD AND GOVERNOR PRINTZ PARK

The site of an ill-fated Swedish settlement thirty-eight years before William Penn founded Pennsylvania

From 1638 to 1655 the area now known as Delaware County, Pennsylvania, was claimed by Sweden and settled by Swedish, Dutch and Finnish colonists.

Printz Becomes Governor

In 1643 the colony, hardly a commercial success, was placed under the governorship of Johan Printz with orders to do whatever was necessary to make the venture profitable to the Swedish Crown. Printz, whose dictatorial manner was reinforced by his imposing weight of 400 pounds, ordered more land cleared for agriculture and asserted the Swedish claim to broader territories along the Delaware to facilitate expansion of the fur trade with local Indians. The Dutch in Fort Nassau, just across the Delaware, at first maintained a cool and detached attitude toward the blustery Printz, but as Swedish settlement and trade expanded, they became openly hostile.

Printz's own home, Printzhoff, part of the expansion, was built on Tinicum Island as a two-story combination house and fort. Several families settled near the Governor's house to till the land.

Swedish-Dutch Struggles

Peter Stuyvesant, the Dutch governor, built Fort Casimir at what is now Newcastle in order to challenge the increasing dominance of the brash Swede. Despairing of his ability to contest the Dutch without increased support from Sweden, Printz returned to his native country in 1653, after which his successor, John Rising, captured Stuyvesant's fort. Stuyvesant retaliated by seizing the entire Swedish colony in 1655 and held it until 1664 when the British prevailed and added New Netherland, now called New York, to their empire.

Morton Homestead

The capitol of Governor Printz was destroyed by fire in 1645, and a somewhat elegant structure was built to replace it. Visitors to Printz Park see only the site where both structures stood, but at nearby Morton Homestead they can examine an important example of early American architecture.

Morton Homestead

Morton Homestead, a cabin built in Scandinavian fashion of notched logs, was begun nearly 350 years ago by Morten Mortenson, who emigrated to New Sweden in 1641.

The Homestead probably began as a single log room in traditional Swedish fashion. Sometime before 1700 Mortenson and his son Mathias expanded the house to its present size. A second log room was built in line with the first and the roof was extended to cover both structures, producing what would now be called a breezeway connecting the two log rooms. The breezeway was later walled in with native stone.

Swedish and Finnish settlers introduced the method of notched log building to North America, and Morton Homestead is an outstanding example of one of our earliest surviving log cabins.

LOCATION: In Ephrata, Lancaster County at U.S. 322 and PA 272

EPHRATA CLOISTER

The cloister buildings at Ephrata

Twelve restored medieval-style buildings of the monastic community founded in 1732 by Conrad Beissel

Ephrata Cloister, an 18th-century Protestant monastic community founded by Conrad Beissel in 1732, was among the earliest of the religious communal societies established in America. The charismatic Beissel began his evangelical work among the Mennonites and German Baptist Brethren (Dunkards) of Lancaster County in the 1720's. A natural leader (with a particularly strong appeal to women) he attracted a sufficient following to eventually found a monastic community that could not only support itself, but also develop a substantial economy that included agriculture, printing and milling.

Life in the Cloister

There were three "orders" in Beissel's hybrid religious community—a celibate brotherhood and sisterhood and a married order of householders, all three pledged to a regimented life of spiritual purification. The community love feast and rite of foot-washing united members in a regularly performed re-enactment of the Last Supper.

The Cloister buildings that remain, now restored and open to the public, were roughly built of wood and stone along austere medieval Germanic lines. They include the Saron for sisters, Saal (meetinghouse), stone almonry, leader's house, householders' abode, school, malt house, print shop and solitary house.

Arts and crafts, farming, orchardry, printing and bookmaking, carpentry and papermaking were among the economic pursuits of the industrious brothers and sisters. Calligraphic art (called *Fracturschriften*) illuminated their magnificent songbooks and certificates, many of which are still to be seen in the Ephrata chapel.

Beissel devised a special method of hymn-singing and even prescribed a food diet intended to purify the bodies and souls of his followers. At its height in 1750, the Society's membership was about 300.

In the Revolution

Despite their pacifistic rejection of military service during the American Revolution, members of the Cloister voluntarily cared for several hundred soldiers from the Battle of Brandywine.

Decline

Following Beissel's death in 1768, there appeared in the Society no successor with Beissel's exceptional combination of leadership talents, and by 1800 the celibate orders had become almost extinct. In 1814 the remaining householders adopted the banner of the Seventh Day Baptist Church and their descendants continued as a congregation to use the Cloister until 1934.

As a rare example of medieval architecture in America, the Cloister is today an unrivaled treasure. To pass through tiny doors (purposely shortened to enforce a prayerful posture) is a moving experience, and to absorb the finely developed interpretations of knowledgeable guides is to gain an understanding of an unique episode of early Pennsylvania history.

LOCATION: County Line Road, west of U. S. 611, near Horsham, Montgomery County

GRAEME PARK

A grand summer house in the 1700s, Graeme Park was surrounded by formal gardens, and a deer park

This beautiful, simple Georgian design resulted from the remodeling of a malting overseer's house

The Building of Fountain Low

Sir William Keith, Lieutenant Governor of Pennsylvania from 1717 to 1726 and in the Penns' absence their deputy, acquired almost 1,700 acres of land in Horsham in 1721 and proceeded to build several buildings at "Fountain Low"—his name for the property—for use as a malt-producing facility. Despite his effectiveness in governing the colony and cooperating with other colonial governors, Keith was dismissed from his post in 1726 for arguing for a royal governorship to replace the family proprietorship with which William Penn's descendants had been vested after his death.

Graeme Park

Keith left "Fountain Low" in trust for his wife and children, returning to England in 1728. One of the trustees, who was also Keith's son-in-law, Dr. Thomas Graeme, bought the property in 1739. He was a prominent Philadelphia physician who served in government in various offices, including that of Supreme Court Justice. "Graeme Park," as the property became known, was converted from an overseer's dwelling into a grand summer home. The interior of the house featured floor to ceiling molded paneling, and outside there was a formal garden and a 150-acre deer park.

Elizabeth Graeme

Elizabeth Graeme was Dr. Graeme's youngest daughter and the only one to live past the death of her parents. As a debutante she was engaged for a time to Benjamin Franklin's son William, who was later to become royal governor of New Jersey. The engagement was broken off, to Elizabeth's regret it is reported. She later married Henry Hugh Fergusson, a British sympathizer who served as Commissioner of American Prisoners during the Revolution. Because of this, Graeme Park was confiscated in 1778, after which Henry Fergusson returned to England and Elizabeth began a lengthy suit to regain ownership of the estate. She eventually did in 1781.

A degree of calm returned to the estate in the 19th century. In 1801 the Penrose family acquired the property and farmed it until they sold it in 1920 to Mr. Welsh Strawbridge. His family gave it to the Pennsylvania Historical and Museum Commission in 1958. The manor house is of great interest to architecturally minded visitors since it has been unoccupied since the mid-1800s.

LOCATION: On U. S. 422, between Lebanon and Reading

CONRAD WEISER HOMESTEAD

The beautiful stone house of the Pennsylvanian who kept peace with the Indians before 1755

Conrad Weiser, the 18th-century "ambassador" to the Iroquois Indians, built his home in the Pennsylvania wilderness in about 1729 after moving from New York.

Conrad Weiser

Born in Germany in 1696, Weiser journeyed with his family to New York in 1710 and received an early education in Indian customs as the adopted son of Quaynant, Chief of the Mohawks, member tribe of the Iroquois Federation. He later moved his family to the Tulpehocken Valley in Berks County, where he lived a prosperous life as a farmer and tanner.

Indian Policy

His understanding of the native Americans was instrumental in the formation of Provincial Secretary James Logan's Indian policy and was responsible for keeping Pennsylvania free of Indian disturbance until the French and Indian War. An alliance with the powerful Iroquois recognized their control over the Delawares and other Pennsylvania Indian tribes. Weiser worked directly with Shikellamy, representative of the Iroquois, traveling extensively through the wilderness to keep the peace.

During the French and Indian War these peaceful missions were abandoned while Weiser served as a Lieutenant Colonel for two years in the Pennsylvania Regiment, his assignment being to hold the string of forts between the Susquehanna and Delaware Rivers. His home was used as his command post.

Despite the war his Iroquois treaty remained in force, and in 1758 he assisted as interpreter at the Treaty of Easton, where the Iroquois forced the Delawares to retire from the field. When the French abandoned Fort Duquesne near Pittsburgh, the pressure on the frontier was relieved.

Following a brief participation in the mystical society at Ephrata, Weiser returned to the Lutheran Church and became a strong supporter of the Moravian mission to the Indians in Ohio and Pennsylvania.

The House and Additions

Weiser's 1729 house, open for touring by visitors, consists of one large room with a great fireplace and oven at one end and sleeping quarters in the loft. The house was enlarged in 1751, and was later used as an outbuilding after the two-and-a-half-story home was built in 1834. There is also Weiser's springhouse and gravesite located within the park.

Weiser Park, opened in 1928, contains several memorials including a statue of Shikellamy holding a pipe of peace and raising his hand in a gesture of friendship.

The 18th-century home of Indian interpreter Conrad Weiser

LOCATION: Ambridge, Beaver County, off PA 5

OLD ECONOMY VILLAGE

The Great House

Communal living was practiced in this community, founded in 1824 by pious, celibate Germans, followers of George Rapp

For the pious people who left the German Duchy of Wurttemberg, followed vinedresser and weaver George Rapp to social, economic and religious freedom and built Economy (now Old Economy Village in Ambridge, Pennsylvania), Rapp's call to "The Promised Land" was more than a mere Biblical allusion. It was their intention to found a community of brotherhood and love that would prepare the way for Christ's return. They fully expected Christ to walk through the streets of their city.

Rapp, the Leader

From the time of his withdrawal from the Lutheran Church in 1785, Rapp attracted a following among farmers and craftsmen and their families who saw their preacher as a prophet. They were quick to respond to his prophecies and to follow his lead in religious separatism. They agreed to the doctrine of common ownership after they became established in America. Duchy officials were less than pleased with his refusal to allow followers to swear oaths or give military service. Thus, Father Rapp and many of his people, resolving to find religious freedom in the New World, arrived in Baltimore and Philadelphia from 1803 to 1805.

Within a short time 500 followers had settled a 5,000-acre tract in Butler County and named it Harmony. They signed a pact agreeing that all property belonged to the Society. Within a year all agreed to the practice of celibacy in preparation for the second coming of Christ.

To Indiana and Back to Pennsylvania

In 1815, to gain the advantage of water transport for their produce, the leaders bought 30,000 acres in Indiana and moved their people to a location on the Wabash River where their community, renamed New Harmony, grew to 900 with ownership of 180 buildings. In 1825 the town was sold and the members returned to Pennsylvania to be closer to more lucrative Eastern markets. Cotton, woolen and silk mills to produce textiles of high quality were built on the 3,300-acre tract, and dwellings and shops were constructed on about 20 acres of land. Six acres are now owned by the Commonwealth of Pennsylvania, where 16 buildings are maintained to show the social, cultural and economic activity of the old community.

Decline in Production

Differences of opinion focusing on celibacy were exploited by Bernhard Muller ("Count Leon") from Germany, who held that Rapp's enforced austerity and celibacy were unnecessary. When he departed the village in 1832 more than a third of the population (including many of the younger and more vigorous) left with him. Subsequently, few newcomers were admitted in order to decrease the possibility of another mass defection such as that caused by Herr Muller. Without replacement, the number of active members declined rapidly due to celibacy and old age.

At the time of Rapp's death in 1847 (he was 89 years of age) the remaining 250 Society members began closing factories and investing their sequestered capital in outside industry. They contributed greatly to the growth of the new industrialism that was developing to serve expanding national markets. When it entered the 20th century, the Society had a mere dozen members. It was dissolved in 1905 having endured longer than most American communal societies.

Cabinetmaker's shop at Old Economy Village

Old Economy Today

Old Economy Village occupies the center 6.7 acres of the original village. It has been carefully preserved and restored. Here may be seen the Feast Hall, cultural center which housed a museum of natural history and fine arts, as well as an adult school, and the community kitchen, where food for 800 could be prepared.

The shops of the cabinetmaker, tailor, barber, and cobbler as well as the office of the doctor may be visited. Behind Father Rapp's house are extensive restored gardens. More than 16,000 original objects used by Society members are preserved in the village and many Harmonist crafts are demonstrated.

The Printing Press

LOCATION: In Waterford, on U. S. 19, 20 miles south of Erie
FORT LeBOEUF

Museum at Fort LeBoeuf explains French, Indian, and English roles in western Pennsylvania history

Where young Major Washington delivered an ultimatum to the French

Fort LeBoeuf is a reminder of the French and Indian War (1754—1763), which all but destroyed French territorial ambition in America.

An Important Outpost
The French built Fort de la Riviere aux Boeufs in 1753 as part of their effort to link their Canadian and Louisiana domains. This did not escape the notice of British Governor Dinwiddie of Virginia, who sent young Major George Washington to LeBoeuf with a message demanding the withdrawal of French forces. The French refused, and from 1755 to 1758 Fort LeBoeuf was a way-station in the string of French fortifications to Fort Duquesne (Pittsburgh). British attempts to dislodge the French failed until the Forbes expedition of 1758 captured Fort Duquesne. A year later British forces seized French Fort Niagara (near Buffalo), interrupting the line of communication with Canada and forcing the French to abandon Fort LeBoeuf.

In order to guard their new frontier, the English restored the fortification at LeBoeuf in 1760. An Indian attack during "Pontiac's Conspiracy" in 1763 caused the small garrison to abandon the fort, set it afire and retreat to Fort Pitt.

Thirty years later the danger of Indian attack necessitated the re-establishment of the defense system, and in 1794 Governor Mifflin authorized the building of two blockhouses. General Anthony Wayne further strengthened frontier defenses by ordering the erection of a blockhouse at LeBoeuf in 1796.

Post-Revolution Settlement
The town of Waterford, laid out in 1794, prospered as a major stopping point between Pittsburgh and the Great Lakes. Among early settlers was Amos Judson, a merchant who, by 1820, had attained enough wealth to erect a fine Greek revival home. Near the home is the Fort LeBoeuf Museum, which explains the historic roles of the French, Indians and English on the Pennsylvania frontier.

LOCATION: Intersection of U.S. 30 and PA 711
FORT LIGONIER

A museum which commemorates a key bastion of the British during the French and Indian War

The possession of Fort Ligonier was never relinquished by the British in the French and Indian War, and it continued to serve throughout the conflict as a staging area for Fort Duquesne.

Building the Fort
Colonel James Burd commanded a party of 1,500 men that began work on the fort in September of 1758. The work consisted of first building an inner square of about 200 feet to a side with bastions at each corner. In the center were two large powder magazines. In October of 1758 the French and Indians launched a surprise attack on the partially completed fort. It was not successful.

Seven Eventful Years
The army of British General Forbes, ordered to attack Fort Duquesne, moved slowly over the mountains to Fort Ligonier. It included the Virginia regiment of young Major George Washington. The French, aware of the superior numbers of the British force, withdrew without a fight.

The fort continued to serve as a place of refuge for settlers throughout the Indian wars. Along with Forts Pitt and Detroit it remained in British hands during the Pontiac Revolt of 1763. It was officially abandoned in 1765.

A refuge for settlers during Indian wars, Fort Ligonier was abandoned in 1765

The Museum
In the Lord Ligonier Room of the Museum is an original painting of the fort's namesake by Sir Joshua Reynolds. Lord Ligonier planned the Forbes campaign with the assistance of William Pitt.

The St. Clair Room is the only remaining room from "The Hermitage," the nearby home built by General Arthur St. Clair, an associate of Washington, one-time commander of Fort Ligonier, president of the Continental Congress and first governor of the Northwest Territory.

LOCATION: The Eastern area of downtown Philadelphia, several blocks from the Delaware River

INDEPENDENCE NATIONAL HISTORICAL PARK

Located in just a few acres of central Philadelphia are several of our most historic and revered buildings. This is where our nation began

Independence Hall

Independence Hall, the building in which the Declaration of Independence was adopted and the Constitution of the United States was drafted, has become a shrine to the creation of our nation and a monument to our founding fathers who governed during the difficult years between 1774 and 1800. The park was authorized by Congress in 1948 to assure the preservation of Independence Hall and several nearby historic buildings, and is administered by the National Park Service. Its visitors center is on South Third Street between Chestnut and Walnut Streets.

Independence Hall Complex

Constructed between 1732 and 1756, the Pennsylvania State House, later known as Independence Hall, was until 1799 a meeting place for provincial and state government. The Second Continental Congress and the Constitutional Convention held their sessions here.

The Declaration of Independence was first read publicly in the State House Yard on July 8, 1776. From 1790 to 1800, the Federal Congress met in Congress Hall to the west of Independence Hall. This building was originally planned as the County Court House.

Old City Hall to the east, built in 1789-91, was used by the U. S. Supreme Court from 1791 to 1800.

Independence Hall (above) is one of several historic buildings which have been carefully preserved in downtown Philadelphia

Other Historic Buildings

Carpenters' Hall, built in 1770 by the Carpenters' Company, was the meeting place for the First Continental Congress in 1774. Several historic homes located in the park, as well as churches, meetinghouses and synagogues, are associated with men who had a hand in historic events.

The First Congress

Delegates to the First Continental Congress gathered to protest England's colonial policies. Their petition failed to move their British rulers, and a boycott of English goods brought no redress of grievances. Fighting had already begun by the time the Second Congress convened in May, 1775, in Independence Hall.

Soon, to their desire for liberty was added their demand for independence, and on July 4, 1776, members of the Congress adopted the Declaration of Independence. It remains the greatest statement of democratic principles ever written.

The war which followed lasted eight years and, except during the British occupation of Philadelphia, the government and war were directed from Independence Hall. Articles of Confederation were adopted and the first French Ambassador was received.

After the Revolution

The weakness of the Articles of Confederation led to a Constitutional Convention to revise them, and at that meeting delegates labored long and hard to "form a more perfect union." Finally, on September 17, 1787, the Constitution of the United States was signed.

In December, 1790, after a brief time in New York, the new government moved to Philadelphia, meeting in the new County Court House where the first ten amendments—the Bill of Rights—were adopted, the Jay Treaty with England was ratified, and three states—Vermont, Kentucky and Tennessee—were admitted to the Union.

In the Senate chamber, George Washington took his oath of office for a second presidential term. The Supreme Court met in Old City Hall under the first Chief Justice, John Jay.

The Liberty Bell

The Pennsylvania Assembly had ordered a bell to be cast in England in 1751. It was to be used to celebrate the 50th anniversary of the Pennsylvania Charter of Privileges, the democratic constitution granted by Proprietor William Penn. It cracked while being tested and was recast, resulting in an unsatisfactory tone and yet another recasting. Serving on public occasions until 1835, it cracked, according to tradition, while tolling for the funeral of U. S. Chief Justice John Marshall.

The bell's association with events of the American Revolution and its prophetic inscription have rightly made it the most revered symbol of American freedom and independence and perhaps the most cherished treasure of Independence Hall.

Assembly room in Independence Hall. Meeting here, the delegates to the Continental Congress formally declared independence. Later groups directed the Revolution, crafted the rules of government. Liberty Bell, silent symbol of liberties earned by previous generations, now rests in its own pavilion

LOCATION: Both sites are within walking distance of Independence Hall in the city of Philadelphia
TWO PHILADELPHIA SITES

A glimpse of the life of early Philadelphians: Elfreth's Alley and Old Swedes' Church

There are many outstanding old and historic locations in Philadelphia. Two are presented here.

Elfreth's Alley, a street of original pre-Revolutionary houses

Elfreth's Alley
Here people have lived in harmony since 1713—the only street in Philadelphia and perhaps in the entire country to have come down to us in "original condition."

Thirty Intriguing Early Houses
All built between 1713 and 1811, these homes reflect the individuality and style so prized in early America.

In colonial days Elfreth's Alley was a quiet residential street of modest homes owned by tradesmen, craftsmen, sea captains and clergymen—definitely not members of high society!

Searching the Pedigrees
An association of residents organized in 1934 initiated research on the early residents and buildings. Nearly 500 families have been identified as either owners or tenants through wills, court records, tax lists and church registers.

Here Benjamin Franklin visited friends, one of the first Universalist pastors was a tenant, and a black tailor and his family lived during the Revolution. A Swedish pewterer, a Quaker cabinetmaker, and a German potter are representative of the craftsmen who lived here.

Gloria Dei, the "Old Swedes' Church"

The Alley Today
Now designated a National Historic Site, the centuries-old alley will be preserved for all to enjoy. A Museum House which serves as Association Headquarters is open to visitors in summer.

Old Swedes' Church
Correctly called Gloria Dei, this handsome building reminds the visitor of the arrival of the Swedes in 1638. The present building was consecrated in 1700 with William Penn in attendance, and is the oldest church still in service in the United States. Founded by the State Church of Sweden, it entered the Episcopal Diocese in 1845.

Mementos and History
The font, bell, and altar carving were brought from Gothenburg, and hanging from the ceiling are votive ship models from the 17th century. Historic books and silver are part of the collected treasure of the church. America's first clergyman was ordained here in 1703, and Betsy Ross was married within the church's walls—the same walls that later rang to the golden voice of the Swedish Nightengale, Jenny Lind, in 1851.

LOCATION: Downtown Pittsburgh, Allegheny County

FORT PITT MUSEUM AND POINT STATE PARK

The museum depicts the British-French struggle for Western Pennsylvania

Modern Pittsburgh's "Golden Triangle"—at the fork of the Ohio River—was an area that attracted Indians, trappers, land-hungry explorers, and the armies of Britain and France.

So intense was the conflict between the two colonial powers that within ten years four forts were built on the site, ending with Fort Pitt, the symbol both of England's triumph and of the removal of a barrier to westward expansion.

Pittsburgh then became a boomtown, its merchants and provisioners engaging in the business of supplying westward-bound flatboats and wagons.

Fort Duquesne

The first battle of the French and Indian War launched George Washington's public career. In that skirmish, a French force from Fort Duquesne repelled the troops commanded by the young major. In the second battle, a year later, General Braddock was defeated.

It was three years later that General John Forbes finally led a military force large enough to intimidate the French into blowing up the fort and retreating without firing a shot.

Fort Pitt

The British intended Fort Pitt, the largest fortress on the frontier, completed in 1761, to insure their control of the key waterway location. In 1763 the French threat was ended with the signing of the Peace of Paris. France gave up her claims to Canada and the Mississippi and Ohio River valleys. Thus the fort was never put to a test of arms. Later that year Fort Pitt was attacked during the Pontiac Rebellion, but Colonel Bouquet's victory over the Indians at the battle of Bushy Run soon brought relief.

The fort and surrounding settlement became an important trading post, with the British remaining until 1772. It was last occupied for military use in 1792.

Exhibits at Fort Pitt Museum, downtown Pittsburgh, dramatize life in 18th-century western Pennsylvania

The Museum

The Fort Pitt Museum, built on the site of the original fort, recounts the tale of events of the French and Indian War, the outcome of which determined the destiny of Colonial America.

LOCATION: In Bucks County, take PA 32 or 532

WASHINGTON CROSSING HISTORIC PARK

McConkey's Ferry Inn

Where Washington's Revolutionary army crossed the Delaware on Christmas night, 1776 to launch a successful counterattack

To commemorate General Washington's inspirational leadership and to interpret the drama of this turning point in the American Revolution, the Commonwealth in 1917 authorized the creation of this lovely public park.

Visitors find expansive areas for hiking and picnicking, a magnificent wildflower preserve, and buildings of great historic interest dating back to the eighteenth century.

The Memorial Building

In the foyer of the Memorial Building is an excellent copy of the famous painting of Washington's Christmas night crossing of the Delaware River, by Emanuel Leutze. North of the building is a statue of General Washington facing a pool that is surrounded by flags of the original thirteen states.

Not far away is the actual point of embarkation where the boats were launched on that night of high drama.

McConkey's Ferry Inn

Near the site where Washington and his staff camped in 1776, after a campaign that year of continual retreat, beginning on Long Island, is the McConkey Ferry Inn which was then owned by Samuel McConkey, also proprietor of the nearby ferry. It is believed that Washington ate his evening meal in the inn on December 25 before crossing the Delaware to repel the enemy encamped at Trenton. Four days later he returned to the New Jersey side to drive off the enemy once again at the Battle of Princeton and raise the morale of an anxious nation.

The Thompson-Neely House

Needing a building for their headquarters, Washington's staff requisitioned a nearby house, the Thompson-Neely, a beautiful stone structure that still stands in the "upper park" section. It was used for 16 days as headquarters for the staff, with meetings held in its rooms among officers such as General Lord Stirling, Captain William Washington, Captain James Moore, and an 18-year-old Lieutenant, James Monroe, who was to become his country's fifth president. Both Monroe and Captain Washington were wounded during an heroic attack on a strategically placed British cannon during the Battle of Trenton.

At the time of the Revolution the house was two stories high and only one room deep. All furnishings of the building are authentic to the revolutionary period, and many articles of significant historic interest are displayed.

Beyond the Delaware Canal lie the remains of unknown soldiers of the Continental Army in an area known as Soldiers' Graves. Also buried there is the body of Captain Moore, under a headstone which tells that he died of "camp fever" on Christmas Day.

Bowman's Hill Tower

Also in the "upper park," about four miles north on River Road, is Bowman's Hill Tower. It stands on the same high ground as did an observation post used by Washington's observers to search the area for enemy activity. The modern tower offers visitors an elevator ride to the top for a wonderful view of the surrounding countryside.

Wild Flower Trails

Beginning in 1934, 100 acres of the park's land were set aside as a wildlife and wildflower preserve. Its 22 trails, clearly marked with rustic signs, lead past hundreds of beds of wildflowers and masses of azaleas and other blooming shrubs and trees.

Bowman's Hill Tower, left, stands at the site where observers spied on British. Below, the Christmas crossing of the Delaware by Washington and his troops

LOCATION: On U. S. 1 at Chadds Ford, Delaware County

BRANDYWINE BATTLEFIELD

Lafayette's quarters

Buildings, used by Generals Washington and Lafayette, remain in this Chadds Ford site

The Battle of Brandywine, on September 11, 1777, was the first major engagement in General Washington's hard-fought yet unsuccessful campaign to prevent General Howe's forces from taking Philadelphia, then the American capital.

The Houses

Despite the local Quakers' avowed neutrality, some members were cordial toward the revolutionary effort and in fact provided excellent headquarters for General Washington and living quarters for the Marquis de Lafayette.

Washington and his staff selected the farmhouse of Benjamin Ring to house their headquarters because of its proximity to logical Brandywine crossing sites and its ample space for living quarters and meeting rooms.

Ring's property was plundered by the British after the American withdrawal to Chester, perhaps as punishment for Ring's cooperation with the Colonials. Washington later paid 22 pounds, 10 shillings to Mr. Ring as compensation, recording the payment in his "Account of Expenses, 1775-1783."

Less than a half mile north stood the farm of Gideon Gilpen, a prosperous Quaker farmer. Because it was used as quarters by Lafayette, it too was plundered after withdrawal. Gilpin filed a claim for losses which included "10 milch cows, 1 yoke of oxen, 48 sheep, 28 swine, 12 tons of hay, 230 bushels of wheat, saddle and bridle, 50 pounds of bacon, a history book, gun, 4,000 fence rails and a clock," among other things. A poignant meeting took place in 1825 between the visiting Marquis and the 87-year-old Gilpin, by then confined to bed.

Washington's seemingly ill-prepared soldiers were not the pushovers the British and Hessians expected. Although the army of British General Howe forced the retreat of the Colonials, it was at a price in casualties he could not afford. After this battle and that at Germantown, Howe and his men spent the winter in Philadelphia. In the spring, seeing no advantage in their grand isolation, they retreated to New York. Heavy casualties among the British at Brandywine and Germantown, combined with defeat at Saratoga, led the French to sign a treaty with the Americans in 1778. The conduct of the battle is explained in detail by exhibits in the Visitors Center.

LOCATION: In Whitemarsh, southeast of the Fort Washington interchange of the Pennsylvania Turnpike

HOPE LODGE

An elegant Georgian home named for the family for whom the famous diamond was also named

Hope Lodge, one of the most beautiful Georgian mansions in the country, was built for Samuel Morris between 1743 and 1748. Little is known about his family except for his adventurous mother who traveled to England for the Quaker cause and even survived a shipwreck off the Irish coast.

Symmetrical facade of the Georgian Hope Lodge welcomes visitors into an elegant world

Masterpiece of Design

The architect is thought to be Edmund Wooley, the same man who designed Independence Hall. He is known to have been in the area at the time the house was built. It seems to reflect the spirit of enterprise in its imposing exterior, and inside it features molded wainscotings, Dutch-tiled fireplaces, and trims in elegant classical design.

The Revolution

After Morris died in 1770, William West, a Philadelphia businessman, bought the home and used it as a refuge during the British occupation of Philadelphia. His nephew, William West, Jr., may have worked in Washington's intelligence network. Hope Lodge was used at one time as headquarters of the Surgeon-General of the Continental Army, John Cochran.

Interior of 1700s house is trimmed in elegant classical design

Named "Hope Lodge"

Henry Hope (for whose family the "Hope Diamond" was named) purchased the property in 1784 and gave it to his cousin as a wedding gift. The new owner, James Horatio Watmough, renamed the property "Hope Lodge" in honor of his benefactor.

LOCATION: Between the PA Turnpike and the Schuylkill River, south of Norristown via PA 363, east of Paoli via U.S. 202

VALLEY FORGE NATIONAL HISTORICAL PARK

Commemorating the encampment that helped win the Revolutionary victory

In the gently rolling, limestone-topped hills of this beautiful countryside, the beginning of the history of a free nation is remarkably well marked.

A Turning Point
The British were convinced in the winter of 1777-78 that the American rebellion would soon be crushed. In August of that year, General Howe sailed his army up the Chesapeake and invaded Pennsylvania to repulse Washington at Brandywine and Germantown and occupy Philadelphia.

After a succession of encampments Washington's troops, ill-equipped and half-starved, staggered along frozen roads to Valley Forge.

Strategic Site
The location for the winter encampment was selected as key terrain astride the best approach to Philadelphia. Surveyed by French Brigadier Louis Duportail, it was found to be ideal ground for defensive entrenchments and breastworks, which he then proceeded to lay out on the slopes of Mount Joy. In the Park can be seen the location of inner and outer defense works and artillery placement.

In the center of the park is the "Grand Parade," where Baron von Steuben drilled the ill-trained soldiers into a disciplined army. It was here, in 1778, that the alliance with France was celebrated.

Visitors' Center at Valley Forge features audio-visual program and exhibits designed to tell the story of the 1777-78 winter encampment of American troops. Valley Forge received its name from the iron forge built along the Valley Creek around 1740. By the time of the Revolution, a sawmill and gristmill had been added, making the site an important supply base for the Americans. In September, 1777, the British destroyed the forge and mills, and so only the ruins remained at the time of the bitter winter. Memorial Chapel, shown above, is on private property within the park.

A number of buildings of great historic significance are maintained, including the farmhouse where General Washington was quartered and had his headquarters as well. Visitors may also see replicas of the primitive log huts in which the soldiers lived. These rude structures with crude wooden bunks and fireplaces must have seemed like mansions to those soldiers who had not had a roof overhead for many months.

Washington's Plea

Two days before Christmas, 1777, General Washington wrote the Continental Congress: "I feel super-abundantly for the naked, sick and distressed soldiers, and from my soul, pity those miseries which it is neither in my power to relieve or prevent."

As spring approached the health of his men grew. Nathanael Greene was appointed Quartermaster General. Supplies and equipment came into camp and new troops arrived. Word of the French Alliance with its guarantee of military support was received in May.

On June 19, 1778, six months after its arrival, the army marched away from Valley Forge to pursue the British who had departed Philadelphia and were moving toward New York.

Memorial Arch, dedicated in 1917, commemorates the patience and fidelity of those who endured cold and disease and hunger at Valley Forge

LOCATION: On PA 272 north of Lancaster on the Oregon Pike

THE LANDIS VALLEY MUSEUM

Yellow Barn, Seamstress House, and Tavern at Landis Valley. Buildings have been moved from other locations

Three centuries of Pennsylvania farming

Old World traditions survived well in Landis Valley, and their diversity lends great character to this museum of living history, which has been developed on land deeded to the Commonwealth of Pennsylvania by George and Henry Landis, whose properties and collections formed the basis for what has become one of the finest farm museums in the world.

Located in Lancaster County, the museum portrays the lives of immigrants who journeyed to America from many European countries. It has been developed to show the early tools and products of home industry as well as of agricultural pursuits.

Buildings of the Museum

Beginning with a slide presentation in the Visitors Center, one may proceed to the stone tavern building built in Pennsylvania German style of blue limestone with deep windows, divided door and pent roof. In its spacious kitchen is an excellent display of utensils.

The museum has erected a cluster of buildings as a typical settler's farm

The gun shop recalls the day of the legendary Pennsylvania (often mistakenly called "Kentucky") flintlock rifle that was, in its day, the finest firing piece available to any citizen.

In the Conestoga Wagon Shed is a wonderful example of the boat-shaped vehicle that was the principal freight-hauler of produce from Lancaster County to Philadelphia markets. Tool boxes, wagon jacks and other gear associated with the wagons are also displayed.

In the Textile Gallery visitors are greeted by the hum of spinning wheels and the clack of looms as linsey-woolsey, rag carpeting and toweling are produced.

The Implement Shed contains a display of machinery that forms a fine introduction to farming in early Pennsylvania. Moldboard plows, grain drills, and even a reproduction of Cyrus McCormick's first successful reaper are on display.

In the Yellow Barn are exhibits that portray the development of the museum from 1925 to the present, and nearby are

The tavern

restored buildings that house exhibits and demonstrations of many of the rural crafts that were so important to 18th- and 19th-century settlers. There are the Seamstress House, the Pottery Shop, and the shops of the printer, harnessmaker, blacksmith and tinsmith.

Two farms portray the way life was lived in the 18th and 19th centuries in Landis Valley: the Settler's Farm and the Federal Farm. In addition there is a transportation building, hotel, schoolhouse, country store, firehouse, and the Victorian Landis House, the home of the parents of the museum's founders.

Gift of The Landis Brothers

More than a quarter million items were donated to the museum in 1940 by the Landis Brothers, professional engineers of notable accomplishments, who grew up here and began collecting rural Americana early in their lives. In 1953 the Landis Valley Museum became one of the Commonwealth's Historical and Museum Commission properties, then known as the Pennsylvania Farm Museum of Landis Valley.

LOCATION: On Priestley Avenue in Northumberland at the crossing of routes U. S. 11 and PA 147

JOSEPH PRIESTLEY HOUSE

House built by Joseph Priestley, political radical and scientist, is flanked by kitchen and laboratory wings

The home of an 18th-century scientist and theologian

Joseph Priestley, English discoverer of oxygen, champion of democratic reform in government, and an exile in America, built his home in Northumberland, Northumberland County, in 1794.

Minister, Scientist, Teacher

Priestley, a minister of religion with a deep interest in science, was an exponent of rationalist interpretation of Scripture and an adherent of the American and French revolutions. He advocated the teaching of modern history and the use of field trips in the teaching of science, both considered radical views at the time. His experiments with carbon dioxide laid the groundwork for the eventual introduction of carbonated water.

The Priestley House

The liberal political views that he espoused in England resulted in the violence perpetrated by a Birmingham mob in 1791 that all but destroyed Priestley's home, chapel and books. He emigrated to Pennsylvania following the declaration of war between England and revolutionary France in 1793, settled in Northumberland, and spent his remaining ten years living peacefully in the home he had built with local labor and materials. It is composed of a large main house flanked by kitchen and laboratory wings and is an excellent example of 18th-century Georgian architecture with an American flair.

LOCATION: One can view the site from an overlook along U. S. route 6 between Wysox and Wyalusing

FRENCH AZILUM

Susquehanna River site for refugees of the French Revolution

French Azilum (asylum) was settled by French refugees loyal to the king of France, who had fled from the revolutionaries to establish a haven of refuge for themselves and possibly for their queen. Nestled in a giant horseshoe bend of the idyllic Susquehanna River in Bradford County, ten miles below Towanda, the scene is one of pastoral calm bounded by a curving arm of glistening water.

These intrepid settlers from France were joined by others who had escaped from the French colony of Santo Domingo (Haiti) to avoid slave uprisings in that unhappy island. Most arrived after traveling upriver in dugout canoes. Some who came overland from Philadelphia were of the king's inner circle—minor nobility, officeholders, army officers, clergy and merchants from France. Their leaders were mostly liberal-minded reformers whose moderate programs had been thrust aside by fanatic revolutionaries.

American Aid

Several influential Philadelphians who were sympathetic to the exiles also saw an opportunity to profit from their plight.

Stephen Girard, Robert Morris and John Nicholson assisted in the purchase of 1,000 wilderness acres. Within this vast area, 300 acres were laid out as a town with broad streets, a proper market square and over 400 half-acre building plots.

Development

About thirty crude log houses, some with window glass and wallpaper, were built. These were joined in time with shops, schoolhouse, chapel and even a theatre. An impressive "Grande Maison," a two-story log structure, was built to be the site of social gatherings. In it were entertained Tallyrand and Louis Phillipe, later to become King of France. Preparations for the reception of Marie Antoinette were being made when word was received of the unfortunate lady's execution.

Failure

Economic depression in the 1790's ended the dream of the entrepreneurs, Morris and Nicholson. Many of the emigres were disillusioned and drifted away to regions thought to be more hospitable to the French—Charleston, Savannah and New Orleans. Some even returned to Santo Domingo, and Napoleon made it possible for a few to return to France. Only a few French families remained in Pennsylvania.

Dreaming of a home for compatriots and their queen, French refugees from the Revolution attempted to build a haven in a bend of the Susquehanna River

Today's Scene

Not one of the more than 50 original structures remains. Even garden plots have been obliterated by absorption into larger tracts. The serene aura of the original colony, however, still pervades the landscape, and a few millstones and millraces survive as mute testimony to the unrealized dream of the French settlers. The area can be seen in magnificent panorama from U. S. Route 6 between Wysox and Wyalusing.

LOCATION: Between Ashland and Scranton, along U. S. Interstate Highway 81

ANTHRACITE MUSEUM COMPLEX

Four Historic Mining Sites

Within less than 80 driving miles along U. S. Interstate Highway 81 are four historic Pennsylvania sites featuring exhibits that recall days in the 19th and early 20th centuries when coal was king.

Eckley Miners' Village

Anthracite Heritage Museum

The northernmost museum, at Scranton, features exhibits that deal with the effects industry and transportation have had on the economic and social development of Northeastern Pennsylvania. The Museum's new exhibit, *Gears and Wheels*, explores the parallel development of the region's major industries—mining, transportation, and the silk and lace industries—and how each influenced the area's growth and decline. Conestoga wagons, coal trucks, models and machinery are part of the 25,000-square-foot exhibit area.

Adjacent to the museum is the Lackawanna Mine Tour, in which visitors may go underground to view the deep mining of coal.

Scranton Iron Furnaces

The Historic Scranton Iron Furnaces are the remains of the Lackawanna Iron and Coal Company blast furnaces, once the nation's second largest producers of iron. Built by the Scranton and Platt Company between 1841 and 1857, the furnaces were the heart of the city of Scranton until 1902. Four impressive connected smoke stacks are a unique architectural reminder of the past.

Eckley Miners' Village

Eckley Miners' Village is one of only a few original 19th-century planned industrial communities to survive in the United States. It was established in 1854 for the workers of Sharpe, Leisenring and Company's Council Ridge Colliery. At its peak the village housed over 1,200 miners and their families. Today there are 51 original miners' and mine owners' dwellings, two churches and the Visitors Center.

Through its restored buildings and interpretive exhibits, the Village preserves a way of life typical of the Anthracite Region, one that is rapidly disappearing. Inhabited by many retired miners and widows, it is a museum of "living history."

In 1968 Eckley was used as a location site for the filming of the motion picture, *The Molly Maguires*, a Paramount film. The production company built a breaker model, company store and mule barn. Upon its departure the town became a museum rather than an open-pit mine site. In 1971 the village was turned over to the Pennsylvania Historical and Museum Commission, which administers all four Anthracite Museum sites.

Museum of Anthracite Mining

A few miles farther south, along I-81, is the Anthracite Museum of Ashland, which focuses on exploration for coal and on the mining and processing of anthracite. Exhibits include tools, machinery, models, photographs, and graphic explanations of all phases of producing anthracite. Visitors are invited to enter the Ashland Pioneer Tunnel and explore an actual underground mine, and ride an old steam-powered lokie.

LOCATIONS: Railroad Museum at Strasburg on PA 741, south of U.S. 30; Lumber Museum on U.S. 6 between Coudersport and Wellsboro

TWO MUSEUMS OF INDUSTRY

The story of early railroading and lumbering

The Railroad Museum

The Railroad Museum of Pennsylvania displays one of the world's finest collections of historic locomotives, railcars and related memorabilia, spanning more than 150 years of railroad history. From the small experimental steam engines of the mid-19th century through the powerful engines of the steam age, to modern electric and diesel electric locomotives, an impressive panorama of Pennsylvania's railroad history is spread before the visitor.

Highlights of the display include The Tahoe, a Philadelphia-built woodburning steam locomotive, a train of ornate passenger cars from the 1890s and the elegant private railcar of the president of the Western Maryland Railroad.

Visitors may enter the cab of a steam locomotive or descend into an inspection pit to view the underside of a locomotive.

The Strasburg Railroad, a private enterprise, is located in the same area and offers a ride by steam train through picturesque Lancaster County.

The Lumber Museum

In 1860 Pennsylvania became the largest producer of timber in the United States. Pennsylvania's great stands of tall white pine were particularly in demand for use in building ships, houses, shipping containers and tools. Wood was burned in enormous quantities before being replaced as a fuel by coal.

The story of Pennsylvania forests, the lumbering industry and its hardy lumbermen is told in two exhibit areas of the main building.

Reconstructions include a logging camp, bunkhouse, mess hall, locomotive/loader shed, stable, blacksmith shop and a steam-powered circular sawmill, built to appear as they did in 1890. There is a gear-driven Shay locomotive, Barnhart log loader and log cars.

Lumber Museum (top left) features steam-powered circular saw in recreated 1890's mill

Railroad Museum at Strasburg has 150 years of railroad history on its tracks

29

LOCATION: Off PA 419 in Cornwall, Lebanon County

CORNWALL IRON FURNACE

The iron furnace that helped win the Revolution

Cornwall Iron Furnace in Lebanon County, Pennsylvania, is the only such early furnace still intact. Its Gothic windows and soft red and brown sandstone exterior contrast sharply with the inferno inside that once produced cannon for the American Revolution. The Colonials had defied their British masters' restrictions on manufacture, and by the time shots were fired at Concord and Lexington, were producing one-seventh of the world's iron!

The Workers' Village

Iron furnaces once dotted the Pennsylvania countryside, each surrounded by a workers' village typically consisting of company-built homes for workers, churches and a company store. Not far away was the well-appointed home of the ironmaster.

Medieval in style, the buildings of Cornwall Iron Furnace once put out one-seventh of the world's iron

The Ore Banks

Nearby was a rich source of iron ore, the famous Cornwall Ore Banks, surpassed in yield only by the later development of the Lake Superior ranges. In the 1730's Peter Grubb mined these banks, acquired most of the adjoining iron-rich land, and in 1742 established the furnace at Cornwall, named for the English county of his father's birth.

The furnace operated until 1883, and the mines themselves, later owned by Bethlehem Steel, were in operation until 1972, with workers still dwelling in the stone houses of the nearby 19th-century workers' village.

Peter Grubb's sons inherited the property in 1754, and in 1798 ownership passed to Robert Coleman, one of Pennsylvania's wealthiest ironmasters who also owned Elizabeth and Colebrook Furnaces and four forges. His great-granddaughter, in 1932, gave the furnace to the Commonwealth.

How It Worked

The structure was built into the side of the hill to facilitate charging of the furnace. In the upper level one can see the charging platform from which ore, limestone and charcoal were poured into the furnace to separate the iron from the ore. At the base is the casting room, and on ground level the steam engine and giant wheel which operated the pistons that forced great blasts of air into the fire.

Later Improvements

In 1856-57 the furnace was enlarged from 20 to 28 feet square at the base and from 11 to 21 feet square at the top. The water-driven bellows that produced the air blast had been earlier replaced by a blower powered by waste heat from the furnace.

Obsolescence

Nineteenthth-century transportation improvement, westward expansion and technological change hastened the decline of early methods of iron production. Operations in the Cornwall Iron Furnace ceased in 1883. Fortunately, the structure was sound and it has remained as a prime example of the early spirit of enterprise that helped build Pennsylvania and America.

LOCATION: On PA 345, six miles south of Birdsboro

HOPEWELL FURNACE

Hopewell Furnace is typical of the ironmaking communities that set the stage for later industrial progress. Cold-blast, charcoal furnace produced pig iron and castings from 1771 to 1883, went into decline, and was restored in the 1950s

A community devoted to ironmaking

Resourceful American colonists, vexed by the high price of importing European metal goods, soon began to develop their own ironworks, first at Falling Creek, Virginia, then at Saugus, Massachusetts. By the end of the 18th century, Pennsylvania had become the center of the industry.

Iron for the Revolution

Hopewell Furnace, built by Mark Bird in about 1770, is representative of hundreds of communities that supplied iron to the colonies and the young republic. Its furnaces supplied pig iron which was sent to such forges as Valley Forge to be made into wrought iron that was tough enough to be made into tools, horseshoes, cannon and cannonballs.

In an age when most shops employed one or two men, Hopewell employed at least 65. They bought food and supplies in a company store and were housed in company-built houses. After the Revolution, the managers made many attempts to modernize Hopewell to remain competitive, but technological improvements which made possible the use of anthracite and, later, coke, enabled competitors to produce castings more efficiently, and by 1883 Hopewell, losing the competitive battle, ceased operations.

Buildings that Remain

The office store has been restored to portray its function as the nerve center of village life. The living conditions of the people who shopped there are shown in several tenant houses along the old mine road, including three that are furnished.

The 32-foot-high furnace stack, casthouse, water wheel, charcoal shed, blacksmith shop and other buildings have been restored and are open to the public year-round.

Furnace and Cast House

LOCATION: Near Titusville, off PA 8

DRAKE WELL MUSEUM

The site of the first oil well

At the northern end of beautiful Oil Creek Valley, this 240-acre park contains buildings and artifacts that tell the story of the first oil boom. The museum provides an introduction to the production, refining and uses of petroleum in the mid-1800s. Outdoor exhibits include a replica of Drake's enginehouse and derrick built over the site of the world's first oil well, a Central Power Lease exhibit, a standard drilling rig, and examples of early oil pumping and transportation equipment. A gift shop and picnic facilities are located on the grounds, and the Oil Creek Railroad Historical Society operates the O. C. & T. Railroad, which carries visitors on a two-and-one-half hour trip past the sites of the early boomtowns of historic Oil Creek Valley.

Early Petroleum Use

Petroleum, once known as Seneca oil or rock oil, seeped from surface rock fissures in northwestern Pennsylvania and western New York. Early settlers and native Americans used it as a medicine and burned it for light when no less odorous illuminant was available. It was collected by skimming it from the surface of Oil Creek.

By the mid-1840s the traditional sources of light—whale oil and candles—could not meet increased demands, and a search for an alternative began. Refinery experiments produced from oil a product that would burn with a clear and almost odorless flame. Still needed was a large and dependable supply of petroleum.

The Seneca Oil Company hired an unemployed railroad conductor, Edwin L. Drake, to travel to Titusville to find oil in quantity. Drake eventually adapted the salt well drilling technique to oil exploration and hired a blacksmith, William Smith, to help. During their first summer of drilling in 1859 they could drill about two to three feet per day. On August 27 they struck a shallow deposit along Oil Creek just south of Titusville.

Within a few weeks the surrounding valley was deluged with fortune-seekers drilling for "black gold." Hillsides were stripped of their trees to provide lumber for derricks, shacks and storage sheds, as well as for fuel to power steam drilling engines. The world's first oil boom had begun! The cheap illuminant had been found in huge supply, and even more important, a superior lubricant was now available to grease the machinery of post-Civil War industrial expansion.

Enginehouse and derrick replica over world's first oil well is part of an outdoor exhibit which includes pumping and transportation equipment

LOCATION: Just north of the capitol on Third at North Street

THE STATE MUSEUM OF PENNSYLVANIA

Changing exhibits make the State Museum in Harrisburg a must visit at all seasons

A dynamic museum for all of Pennsylvania

The Commonwealth of Pennsylvania's official museum is the State Museum of Pennsylvania, founded in 1905 and located in Harrisburg. Within its curving walls are four floors of exhibits and displays of the state's great historical, cultural and natural treasures. Geology, natural history, archeology, industry, technology, decorative and fine arts, and military as well as political history are covered. The museum building contains offices of the Pennsylvania Historical and Museum Commission, which administers a network of museums and historic sites throughout the Commonwealth. What follows is a description of Museum exhibits, arranged in recommended visiting order.

The Planetarium
When lights are dimmed, the thirty-foot dome of the Planetarium becomes a magic window through which the mysteries of the heavens can be seen. Changing programs present new vistas of our distant neighbors in the universe.

The Hall of Geology
The nature and magnitude of natural history are excitingly portrayed by models, dioramas, graphics, specimens and audio-visual systems that depict changes that have taken place over many millions of years.

The Hall of Pennsylvania Mammals
Thirteen dioramas feature mammals of Pennsylvania. Many of them, including the bison, timber wolf and cougar, are no longer to be found here.

The Hall of Natural Science and Ecology
To provide a clear understanding of the creatures and plants that are found in Pennsylvania, the exhibits of this hall are organized into demonstrable ecosystems: (1) The mountain stream, (2) The lowland stream, (3) The lake and pond, (4) The bog, (5) The marsh, (6) The meadow and old field, and (7) The forest.

The Hall of Anthropology
Inhabitants of Pennsylvania from 10,000 years before Europeans arrived are portrayed in five full-scale dioramas. Weapons, ornaments, utensils and art, found in camps, villages and burial sites across the state, lend great authenticity to the displays.

Gallery of Military History

One of the largest battle scenes ever painted is Rothermel's vivid oil depicting Pickett's Charge, the climactic engagement in the Battle of Gettysburg. Also displayed in this hall are military artifacts including cannon, small arms, edged weapons and regimental flags.

Hall of Industry and Technology

This exhibit of tools and methods of work shows the development of productive power from the use of hand tools to the employment of automatic machinery. Changes through the years in methods of transportation, construction, milling, mining and manufacturing are all illustrated with tools and models. There is a fine collection of old vehicles and even a Piper Cub airplane, made in Pennsylvania.

Memorial Hall

Here, in an impressive, three-storied room is an eighteen-foot stylized bronze of William Penn created by Janet de Coux. Above and behind the statue, a huge mural, "The Vision of William Penn," illustrates the fulfillment of many of the founder's dreams. Replicas of colorful flags and banners associated with early Pennsylvania history hang on the east wall, and an adjacent alcove contains some of the state's most treasured documents, including the Charter of 1681 which created and named Pennsylvania and designated Penn as proprietor.

Decorative Arts

In galleries surrounding Memorial Hall are exhibits of decorative arts and state history. The influence of European design on Pennsylvania artists and craftsmen is emphasized.

Two authentically furnished period rooms are maintained, and a cross-section of building and trade shop facades is set into a lifesize simulated village square.

Cultural and Educational Activities

The Museum sponsors cultural and historical activities in the auditorium, Memorial Hall, exhibit halls, and on the Museum Plaza. A wide choice of school-related events, classes and workshops, based on Museum exhibitions and collections, is continuously offered.

LOCATION: Just west of PA 72, 2 miles northwest of the city of Lebanon

UNION CANAL TUNNEL

The tunnel that was the final link in connecting the Schuylkill and the Susquehanna Rivers

Stonework of Union Canal Tunnel northwest of Lebanon buttresses opening through a limestone hill. Once a link of the Commonwealth's ambitious canal network, the tunnel fulfilled colonists' dream of providing transportation eastward from the interior of the state

Efforts to connect the Schuylkill and Susquehanna Rivers by canal began before the American Revolution, with George Washington himself checking progress in 1772 and 1773. The lack of engineering expertise and capital delayed the construction, and the Schuylkill and Susquehanna Navigation Company went into bankruptcy in 1797.

Second Attempt

With receipts expected from lotteries and some support from the legislature, work was resumed in 1811 and the last link, the Union Canal Tunnel, was opened for traffic in 1827.

Upkeep of feeder dams and repair to locks took most of the receipts of the canal during its 50 years of existence. Leakage due to inadequate engineering and damage suits by landowners were constant problems.

The tunnel is 243 yards long and 18 feet wide. It cuts through a limestone hill northwest of Lebanon. The extreme hardness of the subsurface strata made the cutting difficult and delayed completion long beyond the originally intended date.

Restoration of the tunnel has been done in recent years by the Lebanon County Historical Society.

LOCATION: Along U.S. 22 between Duncansville and Cresson
ALLEGHENY PORTAGE RAILROAD

The amazing railroad that hauled canal boats over the Allegheny Mountain, now a National Historic Site.

The Allegheny Portage Railroad, which began its climb of the Allegheny Mountain west of Hollidaysburg and descended the western slope to Johnstown, was a triumph of engineering in concept and execution.

The Mountain Barrier

In 1826 the General Assembly voted for construction of the Pennsylvania Canal. To link its lower water routes required a method by which 36 miles of Allegheny Mountain could be traversed. The solution was to position stationary engines on a series of ten planes, so located as to be able to haul up and let down canal vehicles. A stone viaduct was built to cross the Little Conemaugh, a 900-foot tunnel was bored, several bridges were constructed and all elements were organized to allow simultaneous passage of traffic in both directions over a 1,400-foot mountain without breakdowns or delays!

The engines that provided power for this incredible system were located in engine houses located on the ten planes. Each one powered a drum on which was wound a hemp rope with a circumference of six inches and a length of up to a mile and a quarter. More than 11 miles of rope were finally used before John A. Roebling in 1843 proved that wire would be superior to hemp. By 1849 all engines were equipped with one and five-eighths-inch wire.

Thirty-six Busy Miles!

Every mile of the 36-mile portage hummed with activity—heavy boxcars, diminutive passenger coaches, small and long sectionalized canal boats, all in constant motion up or down from plane to plane. Wood and coal stations, with firemen and engineers, fueled the engines. Car agents, often called state agents, directed passengers, controlled freight movement and collected tolls. Blacksmiths, blowers, strikers, machinists and finishers were available to forge or repair engine and track parts to keep the entire affair running smoothly.

Obsolescence

During the successful years of portage operation, engineers studied new routes for traversing the mountain range without the use of planes, and in the early 1850s a route completely serviced by locomotives was finished. Introduction of the modern railroad system in 1855 rendered the remarkable canal-portage rail line instantly obsolete.

Lemon Inn at the summit of Allegheny Mountain and the Allegheny Portage Railroad

LOCATION: South of Harrisburg on U. S. routes 15 and 30

GETTYSBURG NATIONAL MILITARY PARK

Farmhouse caught in the action of Confederate battle to advance into the north, July 1, 2, and 3, 1863. Repulsed, the Confederacy never again had a chance to win the war

Recounting the Historic Battle of Gettysburg

On July 1, 2 and 3, 1863, Lee's Confederate Army of Northern Virginia attempted to defeat the Union Army of the Potomac, commanded by Major General George G. Meade. The line of battle, near the village of Gettysburg, Pennsylvania, was near the farthest advance of Confederate forces, and the outcome of the struggle is seen as the turning point of the American Civil War.

General Lee's Strategy
Following victories at Fredericksburg and Chancellorsville, Lee launched his second invasion of the Northern states, hoping for a victory on Northern soil that would lead to a negotiated peace and an independent Confederacy. It was also plain that an offensive across the Potomac would relieve pressure on Vicksburg, Mississippi, then under seige by the Union.

In June 1863, the Army of Northern Virginia, numbering about 75,000 men, marched west from Fredericksburg, through the gaps of the Blue Ridge, then north through Maryland into Pennsylvania. President Lincoln responded by ordering the Army of the Potomac, with about 100,000 men, to interpose between the Confederates and the city of Washington.

Lee, lacking the reconnaissance that would have been provided had J.E.B. Stuart's cavalry squadrons been supporting his movement, did not learn until June 28 that an entire Union army was at his rear. He recalled his advance columns from Cumberland and York Counties and turned to face the new threat.

On June 30, a Confederate brigade sent to Gettysburg for supplies observed an advance party of Union cavalry and retired. The next day, the Confederates attacked and drove Meade's forces to the hills south of town where they were formed into a battle line extending from Spanglers' Spring to Cemetery Hill and south along Cemetery Ridge toward Little Round Top.

The Battle Develops

On July 2, Lee moved against both Union flanks. Ewell's thrust at Culp's Hill on the right failed, but Longstreet broke through the Peach Orchard salient, leaving the Wheatfield strewn with dead and wounded and turning the base of Little Round Top into a shambles.

On July 3, following a two-hour artillery preparation, 15,000 Confederates under George Pickett charged against the Union center, reached the Union line, but failed to break it.

The following day, Lee retreated to the south. Cautiously, Meade's army pursued but made no attempt to halt the Confederate withdrawal across the Potomac.

Graves of Union soldiers

Pennsylvania monument

After the Battle

Lee's forces had suffered 28,000 casualties, and those of the Union 23,000. The Confederate Army was never the same again. Four months later, President Abraham Lincoln delivered "a few appropriate remarks" at the dedication of the National Cemetery at Gettysburg. His words reached far beyond the day's simple ceremony and have touched the hearts and minds of all people who cherish the ideals for which free men have died.

Visiting Gettysburg

The Park Visitors Center is just south of Gettysburg on U.S. 15-Business. Here can be seen a film, exhibits and the famous Gettysburg Cyclorama, a panoramic painting of Pickett's charge.

Available are a self-guiding auto tour leading to important sites and monuments, excellent walking tours, and a bus tour of about two hours. Perhaps the best way to gain an understanding of the battle is to utilize the services of a licensed guide. A tower has been built from which all points of the area can be seen.

LOCATION: In Erie, at the foot of State Street
FLAGSHIP NIAGARA

Deck of the Niagara

A visit will recall Captain Perry's stirring victory over the British on Lake Erie in 1813

On September 10, 1813, an American squadron of nine small ships defeated the British fleet on Lake Erie, removing the British threat to the Northwest and cheering an apprehensive and divided nation.

A Feat of Construction
The construction of Perry's fleet was accomplished in Erie, a small, isolated community with a scarcity of craftsmen and virtually no local supply of materials. Carpenters, shipjoiners, caulkers and others were enticed from Philadelphia and Pittsburgh. Iron came from Meadville, rigging and anchors were manufactured in Pittsburgh and sails were brought from Philadelphia. Cannon were cast in Washington and shot in Pittsburgh. There were no local sawmills, so all timber was cut and squared by hand.

Perry Arrives
In March, 1813, 27-year old Master Commandant Oliver Hazard Perry took command of a fleet whose ships would have to be built by labor that didn't exist locally and manned by sailors who were not forthcoming from the Navy. In the end militiamen were trained to reinforce the understrength crew.

In August, Perry's men began the task of floating the six small ships over the sand bars at the bay's entrance to join the three American ships with which they would confront the British fleet.

Engagement and Victory
On September 10, the British fleet, with firepower about equal to that of the Americans, appeared. The *Lawrence*, with Perry aboard, challenged the largest of the British men-of-war, while the *Niagara*, for a still unknown reason, held back. The brig, *Lawrence*, was heavily damaged but held fast despite 80 percent casualties. Perry transferred by boat to the *Niagara*, now in the line of battle, and as its captain, turned the tide of battle.

Perry then wrote his famous report to the Secretary of the Navy: "We have met the enemy and they are ours: two ships, two brigs, one schooner and one sloop."

The Niagara
The *Niagara* was put to peacetime use, but decayed and was eventually scuttled in 1820. In preparation for a centennial celebration the old brig was raised and usable parts incorporated in a reconstruction of the ship, accomplished in 1913. The reconstructed brig, with her full rig and cannon, looks much as historians believe she did at the time of the battle.

The *Niagara* is a square-rigged ship with 105-foot mainmast. Its 100-foot fighting deck holds eighteen 32-pound carronades and two 12-pound guns. The berthing deck below contains quarters for the captain and officers, dispensary, storerooms, sail bin and galley.

40

LOCATION: On West King Street, Pottstown
POTTSGROVE MANOR

A mansion of classical design with 18th-century furnishings

John Potts inherited an interest in several iron furnaces from his father and began building his Georgian mansion in 1752. It reflects the affluence of a man who expanded his father's holdings to include nine furnaces, planned and established a village (Pottstown), and served as Justice of the Peace and as a colonel on General Washington's staff during the Revolution. He was also a charter member of Benjamin Franklin's American Philosophical Society.

Home of Great Beauty

A painfully long time was devoted to the mansion's construction, since both labor and materials were transported to the site through a densely forested countryside. When it was at last complete, it was regarded by all who saw it as a work of art. Visitors, after a tortuous forty-mile trip through the forest, marveled at its simple elegance, very much in correct Georgian style. The large central hallway is a triumph and, furnished then as it is now, the home's Philadelphia Chippendale furniture found no superior, even in the great cities.

Famous Visitors

Family tradition tells of several visits by George and Martha Washington and the Marquis de Lafayette. The property left family ownership for a brief career as a hotel, but in 1940 it was repurchased by John Potts' descendants and transferred to the Pennsylvania Historical and Museum Commission. With both buildings and gardens restored, the manor is a monument to families who, like the Pottses, brought civilization to the frontier.

Elegant interior of John Potts home reflects determination of its owner to live well on the frontier

LOCATION: on U. S. 283 east of Harrisburg.

HISTORIC LANCASTER

Elegant opera house and ante-bellum homes

Lancaster, Pennsylvania, perhaps the largest inland town in colonial America, is rich in history. It was capital of the United States for one day when the Continental Congress fled Howe's invasion of Philadelphia, and is richly endowed with historic buildings. Two of these are covered here.

Fulton Opera House

America's oldest theatre in continuous operation, the Fulton Opera House conveys the magic and dignity of its great theatrical heritage. Its classically simple facade appears almost exactly as it did in 1860. The interior is elaborately gilded and appointed.

Named in honor of Robert Fulton, the theatre opened on October 14, 1852 with a performance by Norwegian violinist, Ole Bull. Later performers were John Wilkes Booth, Sarah Bernhardt, Mark Twain, Paderewski, John Philip Sousa, Buffalo Bill Cody, the Barrymores and W. C. Fields, to name only a few.

The theatre was "modernized" in 1873 and reopened with a performance to benefit Civil War veterans and their families. It is maintained today as a living historic site by the Fulton Opera House Foundation.

First-class small opera house, Fulton boasts acoustics tuned to the human voice.

Right, top and bottom, Wheatland, Lancaster home of President James Buchanan

Wheatland

President Buchanan's 19th-century mansion has been restored to its original state. Its first owner, a Lancaster banker, named it for its view of waving grainfields. As a young lawyer, James Buchanan bought it in 1848.

After his White House term, President Buchanan returned to Wheatland, where he spent his last ten years writing a reasoned explanation of his much-criticized presidency.

The building next to the estate houses the Lancaster County Historical Museum, open most afternoons.

LOCATION: On U. S. 522, north of PA Turnpike Willow Hill exit
EAST BROAD TOP RAILROAD

Antique railroad cars and a trolley ride

The East Broad Top Railroad is one of the oldest narrow-gauge lines in America and the last three-foot-gauge line in the East still operating in its original location.

100 Years of Operation
Built in 1873, the East Broad Top was built to move coal from the Broad Top mines of Central Pennsylvania to Mt. Union, where the fine grade semi-bituminous coal was transferred from its narrow-gauge cars to standard-gauge hopper cars. It survived as a coal hauler until 1956, and a portion of it has been restored and designated a National Historic Landmark by the National Park Service.

There is an eight-stall roundhouse containing Baldwin steam locomotives, a gas-electric car built in Broad Top shops, and antique passenger and freight cars.

Leaving from the historic old station, the operating train takes visitors on a 50-minute ride through the Aughwick Valley.

Electric Railway
Directly across the street from the Orbisonia station, a trolley leaves for a trip over the Shade Gap Electric Railway. There are open summer cars, a huge interurban coach and city trolleys for visitors to enjoy.

Take a ride on the Broad Top, built to haul coal, now delighting visitors

43

LOCATION: East of Allentown, just south of U.S. route 22
HISTORIC BETHLEHEM

Attending music festivals, visits to city's 18th-century industrial area top list of things to do in Moravian city of Bethlehem

The Pennsylvania city that still lives its history!

During each Christmas season, the community of Bethlehem, Pennsylvania, shares a tradition that started on Christmas Eve in 1741. Count Nicholas Ludwig von Zinzendorf, Saxon nobleman, visiting the settlement for the first and only time, led a congregation in singing an Epiphany hymn that inspired him to suggest that the town be named Bethlehem.

Enlightened Indian Policy

During his 13-month visit, the Count inaugurated missionary activities which were designed to convert the local Indians to Christianity. The settlers enthusiastically took part, not simply by preaching Christianity but by practicing it. They fed the Indians during times of famine, extended housing to their neighbors, and became true friends to the native Americans, who responded by teaching the Moravians how to hunt and preserve game and live in the forest when that was necessary. This resulted in many years of harmonious relations through the 18th century.

Music and the Arts

Music and the arts are very important to the ideal Moravian life, and the community in Bethlehem has always been richly endowed with talented people in these fields. Regular music festivals, culminating in glorious Christmas season candlelight celebrations, attract visitors from all over the world.

Visiting Bethlehem

The guides who escort groups through historic buildings in Bethlehem are often direct descendants of founding families and take great pride in the accomplishments of the community, both past and present. Their museums display the work of great local musicians, pewterers and cabinetmakers. Guides point to the many painted portraits of 18th- and 19th-century Moravians that usually show the subjects smiling. The religion of the Moravian is a joyous part of his or her life and each seems quick to demonstrate that happiness comes from harmonious living.

Christmas Season Illumination

Beginning on the first Sunday in Advent each year, thousands of lights begin to burn throughout the city of Bethlehem, and for the entire season almost every window in the city is lighted by a candle. A huge five-point Moravian star with eight giant rays hovers over nearby South Mountain, and 10,000 beeswax candles are cast each year for Church services during which congregants hold candles symbolizing Christ as the light of the world.

There are always concerts and special presentations of musical programs during the Christmas season. The Live Bethlehem Christmas Pageant has been performed for many years by a society especially organized for its perpetuation. Several hundred volunteers participate by taking parts that help portray the Christmas story as it is performed along with choral music.

In stores, homes, churches and schools there are Christmas "Putzes" (nativity scenes) as a reminder of the meaning of the holy day.

Historic Buildings and Displays

Visitors are welcomed at any time of the year at the 1869 Luckenbach Mill, where maps and brochures are available and participation in a walking tour can be arranged. Here one may inspect America's first municipal water-pumping system, then visit the 18th-century industrial area where settlers developed 32 crafts and trades.

The oldest brick residence on Main Street is open to the public with excellent furnished rooms and a museum shop. There is an Antique Fire Museum with hand- and horse-drawn vehicles, an 18th-century tavern, an apothecary, and two museum houses with wonderful exhibits.

Walking Tour

A walking tour of the old section of Bethlehem can be arranged for groups of ten or more with guides in early Moravian dress. It includes the Gemein Haus (1741), which is an absolutely astounding five-story log building, the Old Chapel (1751), and Central Church (1803-06). One views Bell House Square, God's Acre, Sisters' House, Widows' House, Schnitz House and Brethren's House, all 18th-century buildings.

Bethlehem, Pennsylvania, has become known as the Christmas City, but a visit will be richly rewarding at any time of the year.

Early Moravian buildings

LOCATION: U.S. 322 in Boalsburg, just east of State College

PENNSYLVANIA MILITARY MUSEUM

Exhibits at Military Museum cover years 1755 to present

Saluting the State's contribution to the nation's defense

Although he was appointed "Captain-General" by Charles II, William Penn's pacifist philosophy would not allow him to do more than meekly ask his Assembly for legislation to raise a military force in answer to the King's request. The lawmakers turned him down. His sons did not follow Penn's pacifist theology, but their request to raise a militia was also refused.

The threat of invasion in King George's War (1744-48) was enough to cause Benjamin Franklin to raise, on his own initiative, 20 volunteer regiments for defense. Because these troop units were organized outside the authority of the elected Assembly, they were known as "Associations."

French and Indian War

In 1755, the Quaker Assembly finally moved to meet the threat of French claims to greater territory in the Ohio Valley by establishing a militia, the beginning of a military tradition that continues to this day.

The service of the citizen-soldier of Pennsylvania on the battlefields of Europe in the First World War is commemorated in the memorials that constitute the 28th Infantry Division (National Guard) Shrine at Boalsburg, Centre County. Established by the Division Officers Club in 1919, it became the site later of the Pennsylvania Military Museum, erected and administered by the Historical and Museum Commission. Exhibits that interpret the role of the serviceman in ten major conflicts up to and including the war in Vietnam have been incorporated into the museum. It is open to visitors year-round.

LOCATION: On PA 993, northwest of Greensburg

BUSHY RUN BATTLEFIELD

Remembering the men who opened Western Pennsylvania to settlement

This historic site interprets and commemorates the victory of Colonel Henry Bouquet, a Swiss mercenary in the British service who achieved fame in the French and Indian War and in Pontiac's Rebellion.

The Indians Attack

Indians of the Great Lakes and Ohio Valley grew to depend upon their French allies for much of their food, most of their weapons and all of their liquor. Following the fall of New France in 1760, the British stopped trading weapons, ammunition and liquor. The French had paid tribute with presents, considered by the Indians as rent for land occupied, but the British eliminated the practice because it was incorrectly viewed as a handout. The Indians reacted with deadly force, intended to drive the invaders from their ancestral lands.

Indians attacked, destroying houses and killing settlers. Their siege of Fort Pitt began on July 28, 1763. Six other forts soon fell to the Indians. That the Indians went on the defensive by the end of the year is due partly to their lack of ability to sustain a protracted struggle, but also to a brilliant tactical victory by Colonel Bouquet at Bushy Run. Today a battlefield museum commemorates the victory.

Bouquet's Battle

Sent to relieve Fort Pitt, Bouquet was intercepted by the Indians who surrounded his force of 500 and the supply train of flour that had been destined for the Fort. After a battle that lasted all afternoon, Bouquet covered the wounded with flour bags and then, on the next morning, he deceived the Indians by faking a retreat after which he fell upon their flank, turning the battle into a rout. A year later Bouquet led an expedition to Ohio to take the terms of peace to the Indian leaders.

Site of a victory, Bushy Run also brings alive for visitors the wilderness that was Pennsylvania

47

MAP OF PENNSYLVANIA'S HISTORIC SITES

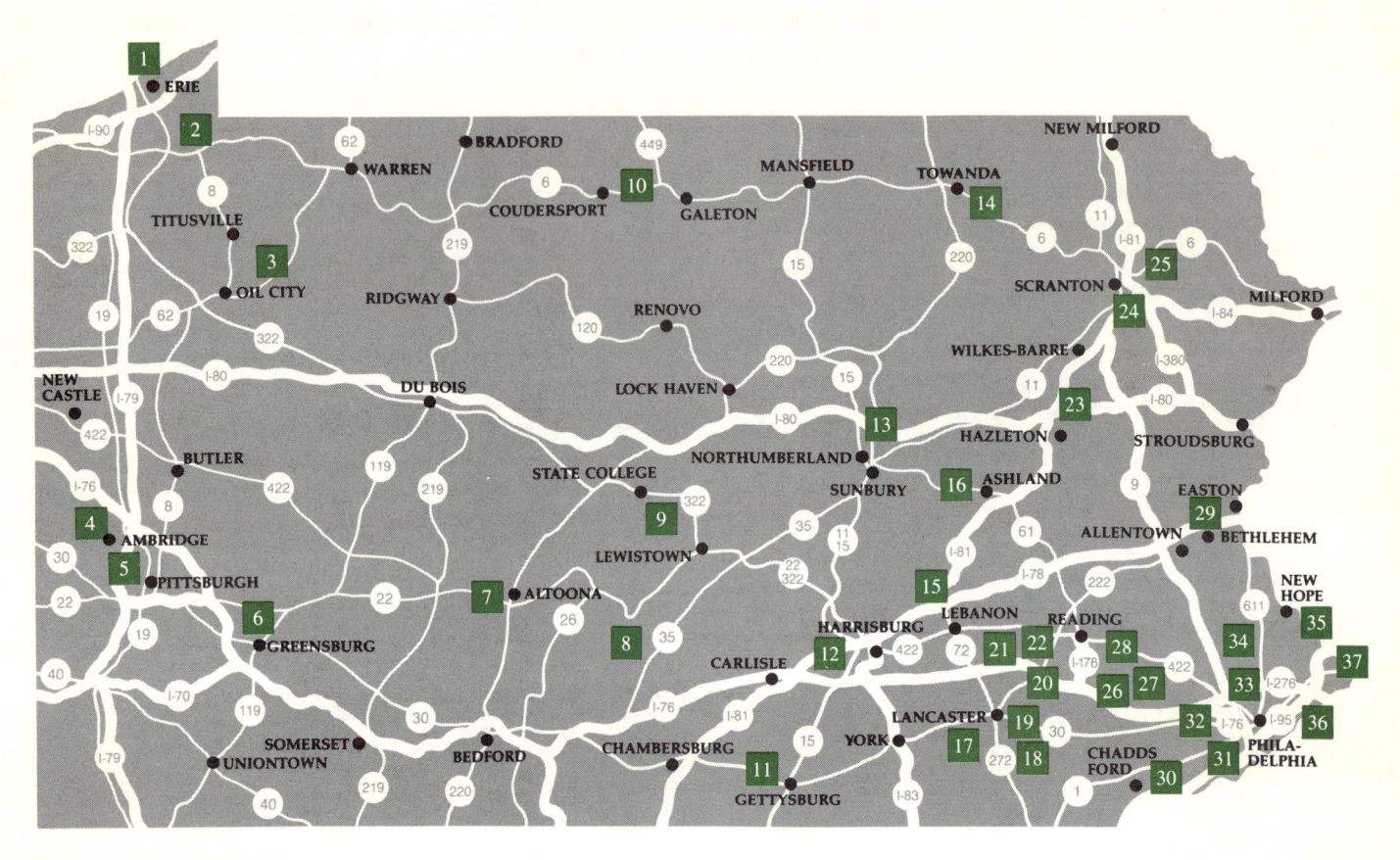

LANDMARK SITES

1. FLAGSHIP NIAGARA
2. FORT LE BOEUF
3. DRAKE WELL MUSEUM
4. OLD ECONOMY VILLAGE
5. FORT PITT MUSEUM & POINT STATE PARK
6. BUSHY RUN BATTLEFIELD
7. ALLEGHENY PORTAGE RAILROAD
8. EAST BROAD TOP RAILROAD
9. PENNSYLVANIA MILITARY MUSEUM
10. PENNSYLVANIA LUMBER MUSEUM
11. GETTYSBURG BATTLEFIELD
12. THE STATE MUSEUM OF PENNSYLVANIA
13. JOSEPH PRIESTLEY HOUSE
14. FRENCH AZILUM
15. UNION CANAL TUNNEL
16. MUSEUM OF ANTHRACITE MINING
17. WHEATLAND & FULTON OPERA HOUSE
18. RAILROAD MUSEUM OF PENNSYLVANIA
19. LANDIS VALLEY MUSEUM
20. EPHRATA CLOISTER
21. CORNWALL IRON FURNACE
22. CONRAD WEISER HOMESTEAD
23. ECKLEY MINERS' VILLAGE
24. THE PENNSYLVANIA ANTHRACITE HERITAGE MUSEUM
25. SCRANTON IRON FURNACES
26. HOPEWELL
27. POTTSGROVE MANOR
28. DANIEL BOONE HOMESTEAD
29. HISTORIC BETHLEHEM
30. BRANDYWINE BATTLEFIELD
31. MORTON HOMESTEAD & GOVERNOR PRINTZ PARK
32. VALLEY FORGE
33. HOPE LODGE & MATHER HILL
34. GRAEME PARK
35. WASHINGTON CROSSING HISTORIC PARK
36. INDEPENDENCE NATIONAL HISTORICAL PARK/ TWO PHILADELPHIA SITES
37. PENNSBURY MANOR